BOSTON COMMON PRESS
Brookline, Massachusetts

1997

Boston Common Press
17 Station Street
Brookline, Massachusetts 02146

ISBN 0-936184-21-3
Library of Congress Cataloging-in-Publication Data
The Editors of *Cook's Illustrated*

How to make holiday desserts: An illustrated step-by-step guide to plum pudding, trifle, mincemeat pie, yule log cake, and other festive desserts/The Editors of *Cook's Illustrated*
1st ed.


Includes 21 recipes and 41 illustrations
ISBN 0-936184-21-3 (hardback): $14.95
I. Cooking. I. Title
1997


Manufactured in the United States of America


Distributed by Boston Common Press, 17 Station Street, Brookline, MA 02146.


Cover and text design: Amy Klee
Recipe development: Melissa Hamilton
Series Editor: Jack Bishop

# HOW TO
# MAKE HOLIDAY
# DESSERTS

An illustrated step-by-step guide to
plum pudding, trifle, mincemeat pie, yule
log cake, and other festive desserts.

THE COOK'S ILLUSTRATED LIBRARY

*Illustrations by John Burgoyne*

# CONTENTS

INTRODUCTION
**vi**

CHAPTER ONE
## Baking Basics
8

CHAPTER TWO
## Mincemeat Pie
10

CHAPTER THREE
## Trifle
20

CHAPTER FOUR
## Chocolate Truffles
34

CHAPTER FIVE
## Plum Pudding
44

CHAPTER SIX
## Chocolate Soufflé
54

CHAPTER SEVEN
## Crème Brûlée
62

CHAPTER EIGHT
## Apple Pie
68

CHAPTER NINE
## Yule Log Cake
76

INDEX
95

*introduction*

Holiday baking exists on its own, totally apart from the everyday concerns of getting dinner on the table. When the brisk, sharp weather brings my family's activities indoors and into the kitchen, I venture further afield, spending time with recipes that I would usually consider well beyond the pale of weekday cooking.

For many, this leads to the outer limits of cooking experience, baking desserts that require sugar syrups or rolling out thin pastry dough. These recipes in particular must be worth the time, expense, and trouble required to prepare them. Guided by this rule, we assembled this book of holiday desserts, all of which merit a little extra time in the kitchen.

We also had to find our way through a maze of recipes that we consider appropriate for the holidays. Yule log, trifle, and plum pudding were obvious. Others, like chocolate soufflé, apple pie; or crème brûlée, might seem a bit pedestrian, but year after year, these classics appear on the editors' holiday tables, so we stand on the bulwark of personal taste.

After some weeks of work, we discovered that these were particularly intriguing recipes to develop because so many variations exist in thousands of cookbooks, some of which yielded quite good results, and others less so. To develop what we considered to be the best, most reliable versions, we engaged in months of kitchen testing and blind tastings. We hope that we have done your work for you, eliminating the mistakes and the blind alleys so that you can have a dependable collection of well-tested recipes for the holidays.

May you, your family, and your guests have a wonderful holiday season.

Christopher Kimball
Publisher and Editor
*Cook's Illustrated*

*We have also published* How to Make a Pie, How to Make an American Layer Cake, How to Stir-Fry, How to Make Ice Cream, *and* How to Make Pizza, *and many other titles in this series will soon be available. To order other books, call us at (800) 611-0759. We are also the editors and publishers of* Cook's Illustrated, *a bimonthly publication about American home cooking. For a free trial copy of* Cook's, *call (800) 526-8442.*

*chapter one*

# BAKING BASICS

**B**AKING FOR THE HOLIDAYS CAN BE A CHANCE TO tackle a recipe that might seem too daunting or too seasonal to make at other times of the year. Of course, trying something you rarely, if ever bake, can lead to problems, and the holidays is not a time for recipes that don't come out right. That's why we have put together this collection of foolproof holiday desserts.

There are a couple of general baking rules that can help minimize your efforts and ensure good results.

**WORK IN STAGES.** Many recipes in this book can be put together over a day or more. Follow the wrapping and storage advice to prepare components before a holiday meal.

■ DON'T MAKE SUBSTITUTIONS. You can almost always substitute basil for parsley in a sauce for fish or chicken. But when it comes to baking, substitutions can be tricky and, in many cases, simply won't work. Follow the recipes as written, using the ingredients and equipment we recommend.

■ CHECK YOUR OVEN TEMPERATURE. If you don't do a lot of baking, you may not realize that your oven runs hot or cold. This is the perfect time to go out and buy an oven thermometer (sold at any store that sells kitchenware) and make sure that the thermostat on your oven is set correctly.

■ USE THE RIGHT OVEN SHELF. When making apple pie, you want the bottom crust to become brown and crisp and not soggy. Since the heat is more concentrated on the bottom of the oven, the pie is baked on the bottom rack. At other times, you want more even heating and should use the center rack.

■ MEASURE CORRECTLY. Liquid ingredients should be measured in glass or plastic measures with a spout. Dry ingredients should be measured in metal or plastic cups. To measure flour accurately, dip the cup into the container with the flour, filling the cup so that it is overflowing. Use a small spatula or knife to sweep off excess flour.

*chapter two*

# MINCEMEAT PIE

INCEMEAT WAS ONCE A COMMON ITEM put up every fall along with tomatoes and pickles. Rich, jamlike mincemeat takes on many forms but is commonly a mixture of apples, dried fruits, spices, alcohol, suet, and minced meat. Mincemeat originated in the Middle Ages, when the mixing of sweet and savory flavors was much more common. Meatless versions date back at least a century and make more sense to the modern cook not accustomed to the combination of sweet and savory.

Our first challenge was to replace the suet with butter. This was easy enough. The filling has a lighter flavor with butter, but is still rich and delicious. We also found that a combination of soft McIntosh apples and firmer Granny Smiths works best. The tart Granny Smiths hold their shape during the long cooking process, while the sweeter McIntosh apples fall apart and help thicken the filling.

As for the dried fruits, we like the combination of golden raisins, currants, and candied orange peel. The dark brown sugar gives the filling a rich molasses flavor and the modest amounts of spice add depth without overpowering the fruits.

Long cooking is essential when making mincemeat. The ingredients need time to cook down and meld into a thick, rich mixture. However, we found that by the time we had cooked the fruit down into a soft mass with concentrated flavors, the pot was dry and there was not enough syrup to moisten the crust.

Many recipes add a lot of rum, brandy, or other spirits, but we felt that more than one-third cup was overpowering. After several missteps, we hit upon an easy solution. We added apple cider, which reinforces the apple flavor and keeps the mincemeat moist but does not stand out. Some of the cider goes into the pot at the start of the cooking time, the rest when the fruit has cooked down (after about three hours) along with the alcohol. We then simmer the mince-meat for another ten minutes or so, just until this liquid reduces to a dense syrup.

# Modern Mincemeat Pie

> **NOTE:** *This recipe uses fresh and dried fruit (but no meat) in the filling. The following dough recipe is firm enough to hold its shape and decorate but still delicious and flaky. This pie is fairly sweet and rich and should serve ten to twelve.*

## Firm Pie Dough

| | |
|---|---|
| 2½ | cups all-purpose flour, plus extra for dusting dough |
| 1 | teaspoon salt |
| 2 | tablespoons sugar |
| 9 | tablespoons chilled unsalted butter, cut into ¼-inch pieces |
| 7 | tablespoons chilled all-vegetable shortening |
| 7–8 | tablespoons ice water |

## Mincemeat Filling

| | |
|---|---|
| 3 | Granny Smith apples, peeled, cored, and cut into ¼-inch dice |
| 3 | McIntosh apples, peeled, cored, and cut into ¼-inch dice |
| 1 | cup golden raisins |
| 1 | cup currants |
| | Grated zest and juice from 1 orange |
| | Grated zest and juice from 1 lemon |

¼  cup diced candied orange peel, optional

¾  cup dark brown sugar

1  teaspoon ground cinnamon

½  teaspoon ground allspice

½  teaspoon ground ginger

¼  teaspoon ground cloves

¼  teaspoon salt

8  tablespoons unsalted butter

1½  cups apple cider

⅓  cup rum or brandy


1  beaten egg white for glazing pie dough

1  tablespoon sugar for sprinkling over pie dough


::: INSTRUCTIONS:

**1.** For dough, pulse flour, salt, and sugar in food processor fitted with steel blade. Scatter butter pieces over flour mixture, tossing to coat butter with a little flour. Pulse machine 5 times in 1-second bursts. Add shortening and continue pulsing until flour is pale yellow and resembles coarse cornmeal, with butter bits no larger than small peas, 4 to 6 more 1-second pulses. Turn mixture into medium bowl. If you do not have food processor, grate frozen butter and shortening into flour mixture and mix with your hands for 1 minute, rubbing flour and shortening between your fingers. Flour

**13**

should turn very pale yellow and become coarser in texture.

**2.** Sprinkle 6 tablespoons of ice water over mixture. With blade of rubber spatula, use folding motion to mix. Press down on dough with broad side of spatula until dough sticks together; gradually add up to 2 more tablespoons of ice water if dough will not stick together. Shape dough into ball with hands, divide into two balls, one slightly larger than the other. Dust lightly with flour, wrap separately in plastic, and refrigerate for at least 30 minutes. (Dough can be refrigerated overnight or wrapped again in plastic and frozen for up to 1 month.)

**3.** For filling, place all ingredients except ½ cup of cider and brandy in large, heavy saucepan set over medium-low heat. Bring to boil and simmer gently, stirring occasionally to prevent scorching, until mixture thickens and darkens in color, about 3 hours. Continue cooking, stirring every minute or two, until mixture has jamlike consistency, about 20 minutes. Stir in remaining apple cider and brandy and cook until liquid in pan is thick and syrupy, about 10 minutes. Cool mixture. (Mincemeat can be refrigerated for several days.)

**4.** Remove dough from refrigerator. The dough is ready to be rolled when it is still cool to touch, but you can push your finger halfway down through center. (If dough has been chilled for more than 1 hour, it may have to sit on the counter for 10 to 20 minutes to soften.) Adjust oven rack to middle position and heat oven to 400 degrees.

**5.** On lightly floured surface, roll larger dough disk into 12-inch circle, about ⅛ inch thick. Transfer and fit dough into 9-inch Pyrex pie pan, leaving in place dough that overhangs lip. Place cooled filling in pie shell.

**6.** On lightly floured surface, roll smaller disk into 11-inch circle. Lay pastry over filling. Trim top and bottom edges to ½ inch beyond pan lip. Tuck this rim of dough underneath itself so that folded edge is flush with pan lip. Flute dough (*see* figures 1 through 4, page 16). Cut four slits at right angles on dough top to allow steam to escape. Brush egg white on top of crust and sprinkle 1 tablespoon sugar evenly over top.

**7.** Place pie on middle rack of oven. Bake until crust is lightly golden, 25 minutes. Reduce temperature to 350 degrees and continue to bake until juices bubble and crust is deep golden brown, about 35 minutes. The bottom crust should also be golden.

**8.** Transfer pie to wire rack and cool to room temperature. Serve with whipped cream or vanilla ice cream.

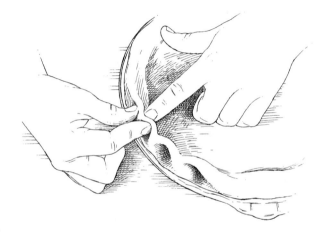

*Figure 1.*

*There are many choices for decorating pie crust edges. For a
double crust pie, we especially like fluted edges. For a small fluted
edge, hold your thumb and index finger ½ inch apart, press them
against the outside edge of the pastry rim, then use the index
finger or knuckle of your other hand to press the dough through
the opening thus created. Repeat this process at ½-inch
intervals around the pastry rim.*

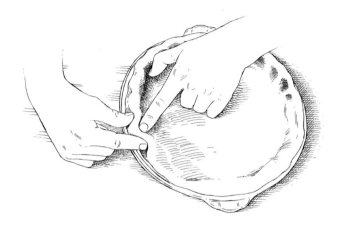

*Figure 2.*

*For a larger fluted edge, hold your thumb and index finger
about 1 inch apart, press them against the outside edge of the
pastry rim, then use the index finger or knuckle of your other
hand to press the dough through the opening thus created. Repeat
this process at 1-inch intervals around the pastry rim.*

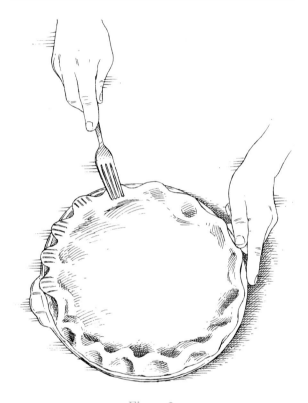

*Figure 3.*
*For a decorative larger fluted edge, use the tines of a fork to mark*
*each large flute.*

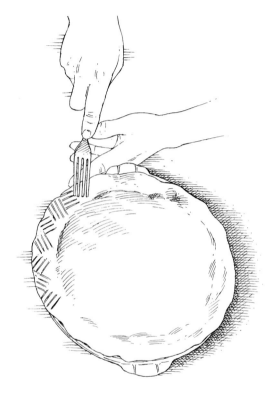

*Figure 4.*

*If you prefer not to flute the edge, make a simple herringbone design. Hold a fork at a slight diagonal to the crust and use the tines to mark the dough. Hold the fork at a slight diagonal in the opposite direction, mark the dough next to the original. Repeat this process around the pastry rim.*

*chapter three*

# TRIFLE

**V**ICTORIAN TRIFLE IS COMPOSED OF THREE OR more layers of sherry-moistened sponge cake, each dotted with tiny almond cookies and fresh raspberries and spread with a rich custard. The top is crowned with rosettes of lemon-scented whipped cream.

The texture of this celebratory dish is delicate and creamy, never heavy or wet, and the flavor is a subtle balance of tart fruit, slightly astringent wine, toasty almonds, and suave, eggy custard.

The custard is probably the trickiest part of the entire recipe. It must be rich and creamy but should not be too runny (or it might obscure the carefully constructed layers) or too stiff (or it might separate into curdish bits when spread over the cake layers).

Most custard recipes that we tested were too thin. We tried using less milk and more cream, more egg yolks, thickening with cornstarch and gelatin, and failed every time. Because all of these custards were made in a pan on the stove, we figured it was time to try the oven and use a water bath, a method that works well for many puddings and custards, including crème brûlée (*see* page 62).

We used a shallow baking dish so that the custard was no firmer at the edges than the center when it set. On our first attempt, the oven produced a thick, glossy, completely smooth custard with the same texture as homemade mayonnaise—perfect for dropping over the cake layers in dollops.

The science here is quite simple. The proteins in the eggs need to coagulate when heated in order to produce a thick custard. However, if the eggs are overheated, the custard will scorch and curdle. Cooking on the stove requires constant stirring to prevent scorching. However, stirring makes it difficult for the egg proteins to bond together, and the custard is much softer when it finally sets. When the custard is baked, there is no need for stirring (the water bath prevents scorching), so the custard sets up much firmer and thicker.

# Classic Trifle

➤ **NOTE:** *Although trifle contains many components, most can be prepared in advance. The trifle (minus the whipped cream topping) needs at least 12 hours (but not more than 36 hours) to set in the refrigerator before serving. Once the whipped cream topping is added, the trifle should be served within four hours. This recipe serves sixteen.*

| | |
|---|---|
| 1 | recipe Sponge Sheet Cake (*see* page 28) |
| ¾ | cup cream sherry |
| 3 | cups raspberries, plus extra for garnish |
| 36 | marble-sized amaretti cookies or almond macaroons |
| ⅓ | cup Amaretto or other almond-flavored liqueur |
| 1 | recipe Fresh Raspberry Puree (*see* page 31) |
| 1 | recipe Rich Baked Custard (*see* page 30) |
| 1 | recipe Lemon Whipped Cream (*see* page 32) Candied violets, optional |

**INSTRUCTIONS:**

Assemble according to figures 5 through 10. Serve immediately or refrigerate, uncovered, for up to 4 hours.

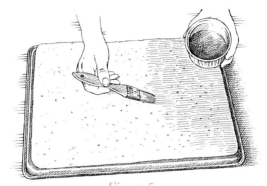

*Figure 5.*

*Brush the cake evenly with sherry; let stand about 10 minutes.*

*Figure 6.*

*Using a serrated knife, cut the cake into six lengthwise and eight crosswise strips to yield 48 two-inch squares.*

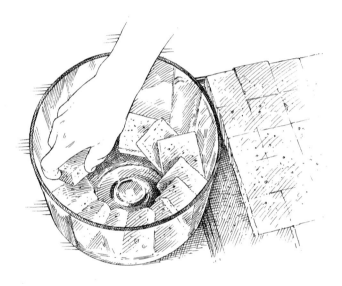

*Figure 7.*
*Arrange 16 cake squares, fallen-domino-style, around the bottom*
*of a 14- to 16-cup footed glass trifle dish, placing 12 or 13*
*squares in a ring against the wall of the dish and the remaining*
*squares in the center.*

*Figure 8.*
Tuck two or three raspberries between each outer cake square,
using ⅓ cup total. Scatter ⅔ cup berries over top of inner cake
squares. Dip 12 almond cookies into Amaretto for 1 second, and
then place on top of outer cake squares, near berries.

*Figure 9.*

*Drizzle ⅓ cup raspberry puree over cake and cookies. Dollop one-third of custard over layer, coming to within ½ inch of edge. Repeat steps 7, 8, and 9 twice more to make a total of three layers of cake, berries, soaked cookies, raspberry puree, and custard. Cover bowl with plastic wrap and refrigerate for at least 12 hours but not more than 36 hours.*

*Figure 10.*
*No more than 4 hours before serving, fill a large pastry bag*
*fitted with ¾-inch fluted tip with Lemon Whipped Cream. Pipe*
*large, 2- to 3-inch rosettes over trifle top. Pipe any remaining*
*cream into tiny rosettes to fill in between larger rosettes. Garnish*
*the trifle with additional berries and candied violets, if using.*

# Sponge Sheet Cake

➤ **N O T E :** *Room temperature eggs will increase more in volume than cold eggs, so the whites and yolks are both warmed in a bowl set over a pan of hot water before being beaten.*

|   |   |
|---|---|
| 6 | large eggs, separated |
| ½ | teaspoon cream of tartar |
| ½ | teaspoon salt |
| 3 | tablespoons plus ½ cup sugar |
| 1 | teaspoon vanilla extract |
| 2 | tablespoons hot water |
| 1 | cup plain cake flour |

**I N S T R U C T I O N S :**

**1.** Adjust oven rack to center position and heat oven to 350 degrees. Lightly grease 18-by-11-inch jelly roll pan or 16-by-12-inch half sheet pan. Line bottom and sides of pan with wax paper, allowing 1-inch overhang on each end. Do not grease paper.

**2.** Place egg whites in large bowl and warm to room temperature over pan of hot water. Remove bowl with whites from hot water and whip with electric mixer at medium speed until foamy. Add cream of tartar and salt, increase mixer speed to medium-high, and beat whites to soft but definite peaks. Slowly sprinkle in 3 tablespoons sugar; continue to beat until whites are shiny and very thick, 3 to 4 minutes. Scrape whites into wide 4-quart mixing bowl.

**3.** Without washing bowl or beaters, add yolks. Warm to room temperature over pan of hot water. Remove bowl with yolks from hot water. Add vanilla and hot water; beat at high speed for 1 minute. Slowly add remaining ½ cup sugar; beat until mixture is pale, shiny, and almost as thick as marshmallow cream, 4 to 5 minutes longer.

**4.** Scrape yolk mixture over egg whites; gently fold with rubber spatula until about two-thirds mixed. Sift flour over egg mixture; gently fold until flour is completely incorporated. Spread batter into prepared pan, smoothing top with spatula. Bake until cake top is lightly browned and center springs back when lightly pressed, 12 to 15 minutes.

**5.** Remove pan from oven and immediately free cake edges from pan sides with knife. Smooth sheet of wax paper over cake top. Place another sheet pan or cookie sheet on top of cake. Flip over both pans and lift off baking pan with cake. Cool cake, then gently peel off wax paper from cake bottom, removing bottom crust. Flip cake, top side up, then peel off second sheet of wax paper, removing top crust. (Cake can be wrapped in plastic, then foil, and refrigerated for 1 day.)

# Rich Baked Custard

➤ **NOTE**: *A glass baking dish such as Pyrex is essential for this recipe.*

| | |
|---:|---|
| 12 | large egg yolks |
| 1 | cup sugar |
| ½ | teaspoon freshly grated nutmeg |
| 2 | cups milk |
| 1 | cup heavy cream |
| ¼ | cup brandy or Cognac |

**INSTRUCTIONS:**

**1.** Adjust oven rack to center position and heat oven to 300 degrees. Line bottom of large deep roasting pan with kitchen towel. Set 13-by-9-inch glass baking dish in roasting pan. Bring a kettle of water to boil.

**2.** Whisk yolks, sugar, and nutmeg together in large bowl. Meanwhile, bring milk and cream to gentle simmer in large saucepan, stirring frequently to prevent boiling over. Slowly whisk milk mixture into yolks; stir in brandy. Set roasting pan in oven; pour custard into baking dish. Pour enough boiling water into roasting pan to reach custard's height. Cover roasting pan with heavy-duty aluminum foil.

**3.** Bake custard until spoonful taken from center is texture of soft yogurt, 45 to 55 minutes. Remove roasting pan from oven, remove foil, and allow custard to cool until tepid in water bath. Remove glass baking dish from water bath, cover with plastic wrap, and refrigerate until cold. (Custard can be refrigerated overnight.)

# Fresh Raspberry Puree

➢ **NOTE:** *Thawed frozen raspberries can be used if fresh are not available. This recipe makes about 1 cup.*

2   **cups raspberries**
3   **tablespoons sugar**

**INSTRUCTIONS:**

Puree berries and sugar in blender or food processor fitted with metal blade. Strain through fine sieve, pressing on solids to release juice; discard seeds. (Puree can be covered and refrigerated for 1 day.)

# Lemon Whipped Cream

➤ **NOTE:** *The lemon zest needs time to infuse the cream, so prepare at least 12 hours before using. Just before assembling trifle, strain cream and whip to stiff peaks. A food processor does the best job of grinding the zest and sugar very fine. However, you can do this by hand, mincing the zest with 1 tablespoon or so of sugar on a cutting board with a chef's knife. Mix the minced zest with the rest of the sugar, whisk in the lemon juice, and proceed as directed in the recipe.*

| | |
|---|---|
| 3 | medium lemons, washed with warm water and dried |
| ½ | cup sugar |
| 2 | cups heavy cream |
| 2 | tablespoons cream sherry |

▪▪ **INSTRUCTIONS:**

**1.** Remove lemon zest with vegetable peeler. Squeeze, then strain enough juice to make ½ cup.

**2.** Finely grind zest and sugar in food processor fitted with metal blade, about 2 minutes. With machine running, gradually dribble in lemon juice. Scrape mixture into airtight container. Whisk in cream and sherry, cover tightly, and refrigerate until mixture is thick and lemon-flavored, at least 12 hours but not more than 36 hours.

**3.** Strain cream mixture through fine-mesh sieve and into large bowl, pressing on zest to release cream. Whip cream with electric mixer on medium-high speed to stiff peaks. Pipe immediately over trifle.

*chapter four*

# CHOCOLATE TRUFFLES

THE PERFECT TRUFFLE IS A BALANCED amalgam of texture and flavor that produces the ultimate chocolate experience. The predominant flavor should be chocolate, with other ingredients added only as enhancers. The texture should be sensuously creamy and light, despite its richness. The chocolate coating should be thin and delicate, just thick enough to keep the creamy center from losing its shape.

Truffle centers are made from a mixture of cream and chocolate called ganache. Many ganache recipes call for pouring hot cream into a bowl with chopped chocolate, but

**3 4**

some chocolate may not melt with this method, giving the filling a grainy texture. We find that melting the chocolate, either in the microwave or in a bowl set over a pan of gently simmering water, and then combining it with warm cream is more reliable.

In addition to chocolate and cream, we found that adding a little butter improved the texture of the ganache because its melting temperature is lower than that of chocolate and hence the mouth feel of the truffles is improved. However, too much butter will make the ganache dense and heavy tasting, so limit butter to 2 ounces per pound of chocolate.

A little corn syrup boosts the sweetness of the truffles and makes the filling even more smooth. Again, too much corn syrup should be avoided because it can cause gumminess.

The other major challenge in preparing truffles is the chocolate shell. Tempering chocolate is very complicated and dipping, unless done by a professional, usually results in a thick coating. We prefer to dip our hands right into the melted chocolate and then roll the truffle centers in our hands to give them a light coating. The truffles are then rolled in cocoa powder, which hides any imperfections.

# Easy Chocolate Truffles

➤ **NOTE**: *Although brandy or Cognac is traditional, use rum or any flavored liqueur, such as Amaretto, Frangelico, or Kirsch, in the chocolate centers. Melt the chocolate for centers in a bowl set over a pan of gently simmering water or in a microwave at 50 percent power, stirring every minute or so, until smooth. This recipe makes three or four dozen small truffles. See figures 11 through 17, page 38, for tips on shaping truffles.*

## Chocolate Centers

- ½ cup heavy cream
- 2 tablespoons unsalted butter
- 1 tablespoon light corn syrup
- 9 ounces semisweet or bittersweet chocolate, chopped
- 2 tablespoons brandy, Cognac, rum, or liqueur

## Chocolate Coating

- 12 ounces semisweet or bittersweet chocolate, chopped
- 2 cups Dutch-process cocoa powder, sifted into baking pan

**36**

**INSTRUCTIONS:**

**1.** Combine cream, butter, and corn syrup in small saucepan and bring to simmer over low heat. Remove from heat and cool for 5 minutes.

**2.** Melt 9 ounces chocolate in large bowl and whisk in cooled cream mixture until smooth. Whisk in alcohol. Cool mixture to room temperature, 1 to 2 hours.

**3.** Whip chocolate mixture with electric mixer until it thickens a bit, about 30 seconds. Do not overwhip or mixture will harden and become grainy. Scrape mixture into pastry bag fitted with ½-inch plain tube. Pipe out 1-inch spheres onto baking sheet lined with parchment or wax paper. Refrigerate centers until firm, at least 1 hour.

**4.** To coat truffles, melt 12 ounces chocolate and allow to cool to 90 degrees. Coat centers with thin layer of chocolate by dipping hand in chocolate and rubbing centers across palm. Deposit truffles in pan filled with sifted cocoa. Use fork to roll truffle in cocoa; leave in pan until outsides are set, about 2 minutes. Transfer truffles to clean pan. When completely firm, place several truffles at a time in strainer and roll to remove excess cocoa. Place in airtight container and refrigerate for up to 1 week.

*Figure 11.*

*Fill a pastry bag fitted with ½-inch plain tube with whipped chocolate mixture. Holding bag perpendicular to and about 1 inch above a baking sheet lined with parchment or wax paper, squeeze top of bag to push out a small sphere of chocolate. After the sphere forms, stop squeezing and pull tube away to the side to avoid leaving a long tail.*

*Figure 12.*
*If you don't have a pastry bag, use the bowl on a melon baller or a*
*small scoop that measures just under a tablespoon to scoop out*
*pieces of ganache and carefully set them on the paper-lined baking*
*sheet. Scooped truffles will be knobby, not round like piped truffles.*

*Figure 13.*

*Dipping truffle centers into melted chocolate often results in a thick coating of chocolate. The following method is a bit messy but guarantees a thin, delicate coating. Start by arranging a baking sheet with chilled centers, a bowl with melted chocolate, and a baking pan filled with sifted cocoa on a work surface. Dip flat palm of one hand about ¼-inch deep into bowl of melted chocolate.*

*Figure 14.*
*Pick up truffle center with clean hand.*

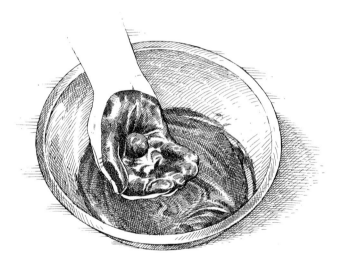

*Figure 15.*

*Transfer truffle to chocolate-covered hand, and close hand around
center to coat it with chocolate. Drop coated truffle into the cocoa.
Do this with 2 or 3 more truffle centers before redipping
hand in chocolate.*

*Figure 16.*

As soon as truffles are in the pan with the cocoa, roll them
around using a fork in your clean hand. Better yet, have a second
person do this. Leave truffles in pan with cocoa until set and
then transfer with fork or clean fingers to clean pan.

*Figure 17.*

When completely firm, place 5 or 6 truffles in a strainer and
gently roll around to dislodge any excess cocoa. Place truffles in
airtight container and refrigerate until ready to serve.

*chapter five*

# PLUM PUDDING

**P**LUM PUDDING IS THE CLASSIC ENGLISH DESSERT for Christmas. Like other steamed puddings, this cake-like confection has a dense texture that is especially moist. The flavors are rich and concentrated, with spices and dried fruits predominating.

While traditional recipes call for suet, we wanted to use butter because suet can be difficult (if not impossible) to locate in many parts of the country. The color is not quite as dark when the pudding is made with butter, and the texture is a bit more crumbly, but otherwise the results are the same.

In England, Christmas pudding and other steamed

puddings are commonly prepared in ceramic pudding basins, which are essentially, deep, steep-sided bowls that often come with lids and handles. Fancy fluted tube (or "steeple") molds, which also usually come with snap-on lids, are available in a number of sizes and produce particularly attractive steamed puddings. Tube molds come in both metal and ceramic; metal ones tend to promote sticking, but are serviceable if you smooth a patch of foil flush against the greased bottom.

Although a mold with a cover and handle will make maneuvering the pudding in the steamer easier, it is not essential. Any large heatproof glass or ceramic bowl can be used to make plum pudding.

Whether you use a bowl or a mold, plum pudding needs to be cooked on top of the stove in a tightly covered pot containing enough simmering water to reach halfway up the sides of the pudding mold. We say that the pudding is steamed, but because steaming, today, usually implies cooking something over, not in, boiling water, it might be more accurate to say that the pudding is boiled. Do not be intimated by this unfamiliar cooking procedure—it's easy, flexible, and quite forgiving of error. Just remember to add more boiling water as needed to prevent the pot from running dry during the long steaming process.

# Plum Pudding

➤ **NOTE:** *Choose any large pot for steaming the pudding. Just make sure that the pot is tall enough to be tightly covered once the pudding is inside, and remember that there will be a rack underneath the pudding as well as a cover or plate over the mold. Remember, too, that the steamer must be roomy enough to allow you to reach in and extract the cooked pudding, your hands protected by mitts or rubber gloves. Of course, a pudding mold with a handle makes the job easier. This recipe serves sixteen. See figures 18 through 21, page 49, for tips on making plum pudding.*

| | |
|---|---|
| 2⅔ | cups (1 pound) dark raisins |
| 2 | cups (10 ounces) dried currants |
| 2 | cups water |
| 1 | cup plain bread crumbs |
| ¾ | cup all-purpose flour |
| 1 | cup (8 ounces) firmly packed dark brown sugar |
| 2 | teaspoons ground cinnamon |
| 2 | teaspoons ground ginger |
| ½ | teaspoon ground cloves |
| 1 | teaspoon salt |
| ½ | pound (2 sticks) chilled unsalted butter, cut into ¼-inch bits |
| 4 | large eggs |
| ⅓ | cup brandy or Cognac |
| ½ | cup sweet sherry (cream or Amontillado) |

**46**

¼  cup (2 ounces) finely chopped citron, optional
    Vegetable shortening for greasing mold
¼  cup additional brandy or Cognac for
    flaming the pudding, optional

**INSTRUCTIONS:**

**1.** Chop half the raisins into pieces roughly the same size as currants. Combine chopped and whole raisins and currants in large, heavy-bottomed pot; add water. Cover and bring to boil; uncover and simmer briskly, stirring frequently, until nearly all liquid has evaporated, 15 to 18 minutes. Remove pot from heat, recover, and let cool to room temperature, at least 2 hours.

**2.** Combine bread crumbs, flour, brown sugar, spices, and salt in workbowl of food processor fitted with metal blade. Process until brown sugar is completely pulverized. Add butter and pulse until mixture is consistency of coarse bread crumbs. Be careful not to allow mixture to clump. Whisk eggs in large bowl until foamy, then beat in brandy and sherry. Stir in crumb mixture. Add cooked fruits and their juices and optional citron, and stir until well blended.

**3.** Very thickly grease 2½- or 3-quart mold with shortening. Turn pudding batter into mold, leaving at least ¾ inch space between top of batter and rim of mold for expansion during steaming. If mold comes with cover, grease inside of cover and snap it in place. Otherwise, crimp sheet of heavy-duty aluminum foil over rim of mold with as little overhang as possible down sides. (Water tends to climb up overhanging foil.)

**4.** Arrange cake rack in bottom of large pot and set mold on top. Pour enough boiling water into pot to come halfway up sides of mold. If mold does not have its own cover, place upside-down plate over foil and cover pot. Turn heat to high and return water to boil as quickly as possible to set outside of pudding and prevent sticking. Lower heat to maintain brisk simmer and steam for 3½ hours, replenishing pot with additional boiling water as needed.

**5.** Remove mold from pot and let pudding cool until tepid. Shake mold back and forth to loosen pudding, then unmold onto large sheet of heavy-duty foil. Wrap pudding tightly, then wrap in second sheet of foil or enclose in zipper-lock plastic bag. Let pudding stand at cool room temperature for 3 days, then refrigerate for at least 1 week and up to 2 months.

**6.** When ready to serve, return pudding to original mold that has been well greased and steam 2 to 3 hours, until center registers 160 degrees on instant read thermometer, or knife plunged in center comes out hot. (Once reheated, pudding can be left in pot, with heat shut off, for 1 to 2 hours before serving). Invert pudding onto platter and unmold. If you wish to flame pudding, warm brandy in small saucepan until barely tepid. Drizzle brandy over pudding, and then, standing back, ignite with long wooden match. Cut into wedges and serve with hard sauce.

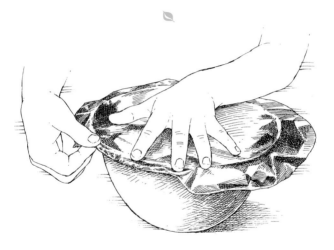

*Figure 18.*
*Fill a well-greased mold with pudding batter, leaving at least ¾ inch of space between the batter and rim to allow for expansion. If the mold comes with a cover, grease the inside of cover and snap it in place. Otherwise, cut a piece of heavy-duty foil 1 inch larger than mold. Crimp foil over the rim of the mold with as little overhang as possible down sides, because water tends to travel up overhanging foil.*

*Figure 19.*
Arrange a cake rack on the bottom of the steamer to protect the
pudding from direct contact with the heat. Place the mold in the
steamer and carefully add boiling water to come halfway up the
sides of the mold.

*Figure 20.*
*If the mold does not have its own cover, place an upside-down*
*plate over foil. Steam for 3½ hours.*

**51**

*Figure 21.*

*Remove mold from pot and let pudding cool until tepid. Shake mold back and forth to loosen pudding, then unmold onto large sheet of foil. Wrap pudding tightly in foil, then wrap in second sheet of foil or enclose in zipper-lock plastic bag.*

# Fluffy Orange-Mace Hard Sauce

➤ **NOTE:** *The secret to this sauce is to add the spirits quite slowly; otherwise, the sauce may thin out. Use lemon zest in place of orange if desired.*

½ **pound (2 sticks) unsalted butter, softened**

3 **cups confectioners' sugar**

**Grated zest of 1 large orange**

½ **teaspoon ground mace**

¼ **teaspoon salt**

⅓ **cup brandy or Cognac**

2 **tablespoons sweet sherry (cream or Amontillado)**

**INSTRUCTIONS:**

**1.** Combine butter, sugar, zest, mace, and salt in large bowl with electric mixer set at low speed; gradually increase speed to medium-high and beat until mixture is fluffy and looks almost white, 7 to 10 minutes. Scrape down sides of bowl.

**2.** Combine brandy and sherry in measuring cup. With mixer running, very slowly dribble in spirits until well combined. Turn mixture into airtight container and refrigerate for up to 1 week. Bring refrigerated sauce to room temperature before transferring to serving dish or it will separate.

*chapter six*

# CHOCOLATE SOUFFLÉ

THE PERFECT SOUFFLÉ HAS A CRUSTY exterior, a dramatic rise above the rim, an airy but substantial outer layer, and a rich, loose center that is not completely set. A great chocolate soufflé must also convey strong, clear chocolate flavor.

A primary consideration when trying to create such a soufflé is the base, the mixture that gives substance and flavor to the soufflé as opposed to the lift and airiness provided by the beaten egg whites. In our testing, we found that egg yolks beaten with sugar are better than the classic béchamel (butter, flour, and milk) or pastry cream (egg yolks beaten with sugar and then heated with milk).

Without any milk, which can block out other flavors, the chocolate notes come through loud and clear.

The other key is the egg whites. We found that adding two more whites than yolks prevents the outside layer from becoming too cakey (a problem with most chocolate soufflés) and also gives better lift.

One factor we found to be of surprising importance was the baking dish. We tried using a standard casserole dish and the soufflé rose right out of the dish and onto the oven floor. Whether using a single large soufflé dish or eight individual ramekins, the sides must be perfectly straight.

We also wanted to develop a soufflé base that could be prepared ahead of time and then baked as needed. Because beaten egg whites lose volume quickly, this is harder than it sounds. We tried refrigerating and freezing our basic soufflé batter and found that freezing portions in individual ramekins rather than a large dish worked best, although the rise was not as dramatic as we like. Adding confectioners' sugar to the beaten whites helped stabilize them and keep the rise high. We also added hot sugar syrup to the yolks to increase their volume, instead of plain sugar.

There are three ways to know when a chocolate soufflé is done—when you can smell the chocolate, when the soufflé stops rising, and when only the center jiggles when the dish is gently shaken.

# Chocolate Soufflé

> **N O T E :** *If you prefer, make one large soufflé in a buttered and sugared 2-quart soufflé dish and bake for about 25 minutes. If you like, melt the chocolate in a microwave set at 50 percent power for three minutes, stirring in the butter after two minutes. This recipe serves eight.*

| | |
|---|---|
| 5 | tablespoons unsalted butter (1 tablespoon softened, remaining 4 tablespoons cut into ½-inch chunks) |
| 1 | tablespoon plus ⅓ cup sugar |
| 8 | ounces bittersweet or semisweet chocolate, chopped coarse |
| ⅛ | teaspoon salt |
| ½ | teaspoon vanilla extract |
| 1 | tablespoon Grand Marnier |
| 6 | large egg yolks |
| 8 | large egg whites |
| ¼ | teaspoon cream of tartar |

**I N S T R U C T I O N S :**

**1.** Adjust oven rack to lower middle position and heat oven to 375 degrees. Butter insides of eight 8-ounce ramekins with 1 tablespoon softened butter. Coat insides of dishes evenly with 1 tablespoon sugar; refrigerate ramekins until ready to use.

**5 6**

**2.** Melt chocolate and remaining 4 tablespoons butter in medium bowl set over pan of simmering water. Turn off heat, stir in salt, vanilla, and liqueur; set aside.

**3.** Beat yolks and remaining ⅓ cup sugar in medium bowl with electric mixer at medium speed until thick and pale yellow, about 3 minutes. Fold in chocolate mixture. Clean beaters.

**4.** Beat whites in medium bowl with electric mixer at medium speed until foamy. Add cream of tartar and continue to beat at high speed to stiff, moist peaks.

**5.** Vigorously stir one-quarter of whipped whites into chocolate mixture. Gently fold in remaining whites (*see* figures 22 through 25, page 59). Spoon mixture into prepared dishes and clean each rim with wet paper towel; bake until exterior is set and interior is still a bit loose and creamy, 16 to 18 minutes. (Soufflé is done when fragrant and fully risen; use two large spoons to pull open top of soufflé and peek inside if you have doubts; place back in oven if center is still soupy.) Serve immediately.

■■ **VARIATIONS:**

## Mocha Soufflé

Add 1 tablespoon instant coffee powder dissolved in 1 tablespoon hot water to chocolate mixture, along with vanilla and liqueur.

## Make-Ahead Soufflé (either Chocolate or Mocha)

Make the following changes to recipe. Rather than beating sugar and yolks, bring ⅓ cup sugar and 2 tablespoons water to boil in small saucepan and simmer until sugar dissolves. With mixer running, slowly add this sugar syrup to egg yolks; beat until mixture triples in volume, about 3 minutes. Beat egg whites until frothy; add cream of tartar and beat to soft peaks; add 2 tablespoons confectioners' sugar and continue to beat to stiff peaks. Cover filled ramekins and freeze until firm, at least 3 hours and up to 2 days. Increase oven temperature to 400 degrees; bake until exterior is set and interior is still a bit loose and creamy, 16 to 18 minutes. Do not overbake.

*Figure 22.*

*Properly folding the beaten egg whites into the chocolate mixture is key to obtaining a fully risen soufflé. Start by vigorously stirring in one-quarter of the whites. Then add rest of whites to bowl and starting at the top of the bowl, use a rubber spatula to cut through the middle of the mixture.*

*Figure 23.*
*Turn the edge of the spatula toward you so it moves up the sides of the bowl.*

*Figure 24.*
*Continue this motion, going full circle, until the spatula is back at the center of the bowl again.*

*Figure 25.*
*Follow this procedure four more times, turning the bowl a*
*quarter turn each time. Finally, use the spatula to scrape*
*around the entire circumference of the bowl.*

*chapter seven*

# CRÈME BRÛLÉE

PERFECT CRÈME BRÛLÉE HAS A SMOOTH, creamy, slightly eggy custard and delicate, crisp brown sugar crust. While it is necessary to heat the eggs so that they thicken the custard, the risk of curdling is ever-present. Slow, gentle heat is the key to making the custard set properly without any loss of smoothness.

For this reason, the custard for crème brûlée should be prepared in a protective water bath in the oven, not on top of the stove, where the heat is much more direct and intense. In addition, we found it preferable to add chilled cream (not scalded, as is common in most recipes) to the egg yolks. Hot cream quickly raises the temperature of the eggs, something we were trying to avoid.

We tried various combinations of ingredients and found that a simple custard of egg yolks, white sugar, and light whipping cream tastes best. Flavorings such as vanilla and spices detracted from the sweet cream and egg flavors and are not needed. We found that other types of dairy were too watery (half-and-half) or too rich (heavy cream). Light whipping cream, which has a fat content between 30 and 36 percent, is ideal. If you cannot find this cream, make your own by combining equal parts of heavy cream (36 to 40 percent fat) and light cream (18 to 30 percent fat).

As for the crisp, caramelized sugar topping, it is easily prepared under the broiler and does not require the use of a blow torch, as is the custom in many restaurants. Drying the dark brown sugar (it has a richer flavor than either light brown sugar or white sugar) in a warm oven improves its taste, texture, and appearance by removing excess moisture and lumps that might otherwise cause problems when the topping is caramelized.

# Crème Brûlée

➤ **N O T E :** *Use light whipping cream or equal parts light cream and heavy cream. This recipe serves six.*

|   |   |
|---|---|
| 1 | tablespoon unsalted butter, softened |
| 6 | large egg yolks, chilled |
| 6 | tablespoons granulated white sugar |
| 1½ | cups light whipping cream, chilled |
| 4 | tablespoons dark brown sugar |

**❏ I N S T R U C T I O N S :**

**1.** Adjust oven rack to center position and heat oven to 275 degrees. Butter six ½-cup ramekins or custard cups and set them aside in glass baking dish large enough to accommodate them easily.

**2.** Whisk yolks in medium bowl until slightly thickened, about 1 minute. Add white sugar and whisk until dissolved, 1 to 2 minutes. Whisk in cream, then pour mixture into prepared ramekins.

**3.** Set baking dish on oven rack and pour warm water into baking dish to come halfway up sides of ramekins. Bake uncovered until custards are just barely set, about 45 minutes.

**4.** Remove baking pan from oven, leaving ramekins in hot

water; cool to room temperature. Cover each ramekin with plastic wrap and refrigerate until chilled, at least 2 hours. (Custards can be refrigerated overnight.)

**5.** While custards are cooling, spread brown sugar in small baking pan; set in turned-off but still warm oven until sugar dries, about 20 minutes. Transfer sugar to small zipper-lock plastic bag; seal bag and crush sugar fine with rolling pin (*see* figure 26, page 67). Store brown sugar in bag until ready to top custards.

**6.** About 45 minutes before serving, adjust oven rack to next-to-highest position and preheat broiler. Remove chilled ramekins from refrigerator, uncover, and evenly spread each with 2 teaspoons dried brown sugar. Set ramekins in baking pan. Broil, watching constantly and rotating pan for even caramelization, until toppings are brittle, 2 to 3 minutes.

**7.** Refrigerate crème brûlées to re-chill custard, about 30 minutes. Brown sugar topping will start to deteriorate in about 1 hour.

## Pumpkin Crème Brûlée

Combine 5 tablespoons canned pumpkin puree, 3 table-spoons white sugar, ½ teaspoon vanilla extract, ¼ teaspoon each ground cinnamon and ground ginger, and a pinch of freshly grated nutmeg in small saucepan set over medium-low heat. Cook, stirring constantly, until mixture thickens slightly, about 5 minutes; cool to room temperature. Reduce white sugar in step 2 to 3 tablespoons. When sugar dissolves, whisk in cooled pumpkin mixture, then cream. Strain through fine-mesh sieve into measuring cup, pour custard into ramekins, and proceed with recipe, baking for 60 to 75 minutes.

## Ginger Crème Brûlée

Combine 2 teaspoons ground ginger with sugar in step 2 and then whisk into yolks.

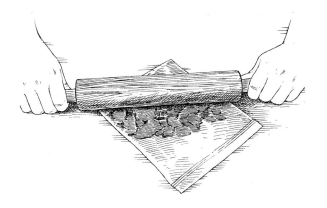

*Figure 26.*

*Drying the brown sugar for the topping in the oven removes
some moisture and prevents burning when the sugar is
caramelized. To make sprinkling the dried sugar easier, remove
any lumps by placing the dried sugar in a sealed plastic bag and
crushing it with a rolling pin until quite fine.*

*chapter eight*

ॐ

# APPLE PIE

B Y THE TIME THE HOLIDAYS ROLL AROUND, many boutique apples, like Northern Spy and Winesap, are gone, and only the supermarket standards remain. We wanted to make an apple pie with varieties available year-round everywhere. After testing dozens of possibilities, we determined a combination of Granny Smith and McIntosh apples is best.

The Granny Smiths hold up well during cooking and the McIntosh add flavor and balance the sourness of the Grannies. The mushy texture of the McIntosh apples is a problem when used on their own but provides a nice base for the harder Grannies and soaks up some of the juice in our pie; it also makes the use of flour or other flavor-dulling thickeners unnecessary.

When shopping for Granny Smith apples, we found it important to avoid truly acerbic fruit. Many Granny Smiths are picked too early, when they are bright green, a color that consumers and store managers prefer. The best Grannies are light green, indicating a riper, more mature apple. In general, more muted colors indicate riper specimens for other apple varieties as well.

With the apple component of the filling settled, we moved on to other possible ingredients. We found that butter competes with the flavor of the apples and is not needed. Lemon juice, however, is absolutely crucial to a good pie because it balances the sugar. In order to give the apples the upper hand, use only small amounts of spices.

In many apple pie recipes, there is a large gap between the top crust and filling, which cooks down substantially during baking. With our crust recipe, however, this is not an issue. There is sufficient shortening cut into the flour that the crust sinks down onto the apples as they cook. This high ratio of shortening produces a very flaky crust, one that is not easily cut into perfect slices. In addition, there is still a fair amount of juice, which we find essential for good flavor, and the filling may spread slightly once cut into individual slices.

# All-Season Apple Pie

➤ **N O T E :** *This dough has more fat than most recipes, giving the crust a crumbly texture that is delicious but not well suited to decorative edging or neat slicing. This pie serves eight.*

## Flaky Pie Dough

| | |
|---|---|
| 2½ | cups all-purpose flour, plus extra for dusting dough |
| 1 | teaspoon salt |
| 2 | tablespoons sugar |
| 12 | tablespoons chilled butter, cut into ¼- to ⅜-inch cubes |
| 8 | tablespoons chilled all-vegetable shortening |
| 7–8 | tablespoons ice water |

## Apple Filling

| | |
|---|---|
| 4 | Granny Smith and 4 McIntosh apples, about 2½ pounds total |
| ¾ | cup sugar |
| 1 | teaspoon grated zest and 1½ tablespoons juice from 1 lemon |
| ¼ | teaspoon nutmeg, freshly ground preferred |
| ¼ | teaspoon ground cinnamon |
| ⅛ | teaspoon ground allspice |
| ¼ | teaspoon salt |

**1**   beaten egg white for glazing pie dough
**1**   tablespoon sugar for sprinkling over pie dough

■ I N S T R U C T I O N S :

**1.** For dough, pulse flour, salt, and sugar in food processor fitted with steel blade. Scatter butter pieces over flour mixture, tossing to coat butter with flour. Pulse machine 5 times in 1-second bursts. Add shortening and continue pulsing until flour is pale yellow and resembles coarse cornmeal, with butter bits no larger than small peas, 4 to 6 more 1-second pulses. Turn mixture into medium bowl. If you do not have food processor, grate frozen butter and shortening into flour mixture and mix with your hands for 1 minute, rubbing flour and shortening between your fingers. Flour should turn very pale yellow and become coarser in texture.

**2.** Sprinkle 6 tablespoons of ice water over mixture. With blade of rubber spatula, use folding motion to mix. Press down on dough with broad side of spatula until dough sticks together, gradually adding up to 2 more tablespoons of ice water if it will not come together. Shape into ball with hands, divide the dough into two balls, one slightly larger than the other. Dust lightly with flour, wrap separately in plastic, and refrigerate for at least 30 minutes. (Dough can be refrigerated overnight or wrapped again in plastic and frozen for up to 1 month.)

**3.** Remove dough from refrigerator. The dough is ready to be rolled when it is still cool to touch but you can push your finger halfway down through center. (If the dough has been chilled for more than 1 hour, it may have to sit on the counter for 10 to 20 minutes to soften.) Adjust oven rack to bottom position and heat oven to 425 degrees.

**4.** Roll larger dough disk on lightly floured surface into 12-inch circle, about ⅛ inch thick. Transfer and fit dough into 9-inch Pyrex pie pan, leaving dough that overhangs lip in place. Refrigerate dough while rolling second disk and preparing fruit.

**5.** Roll smaller disk on lightly floured surface into 11-inch circle. Transfer to back of baking sheet and refrigerate until ready to use.

**6.** Peel, quarter, and core apples. Slice each quarter into thirds, about ½-inch thick (*see* figure 27, page 74). Toss with sugar, lemon zest and juice, spices, and salt.

**7.** Turn fruit mixture, including any juices, into pie shell. Lay top pastry over filling. Trim top and bottom edges to ½ inch beyond pan lip. Tuck this rim of dough underneath itself so that folded edge is flush with pan lip. Press dough with fork tines to seal. Cut four slits at right angles on dough top to allow steam to escape. Brush egg white on top of crust and sprinkle 1 tablespoon of sugar evenly over top.

**8.** Place pie on bottom rack. Bake until crust is lightly golden, 25 minutes. Reduce oven temperature to 375 degrees and continue to bake until juices bubble and crust is deep golden brown, 30 to 35 minutes. The bottom crust should be golden and juices from pie bubbling.

**9.** Transfer pie to wire rack and cool to room temperature. Pie is best eaten after it has completely cooled, even the next day.

**VARIATIONS:**

### Crystallized Ginger Apple Pie
Add 3 tablespoons chopped crystallized ginger to apple filling.

### Apple Pie with Dried Fruit
Soak 1 cup raisins, dried cherries, or dried cranberries (chopped coarse if fruit is large) in mixture of 1½ tablespoons lemon and 1 tablespoon Apple Jack, brandy, or Cognac for at least 30 minutes. Prepare apple filling, omitting lemon juice. Add fruit and soaking liquid to filling.

### Cranberry Apple Pie
Add 1 cup fresh or frozen cranberries to apple filling and increase sugar to 1 cup.

*Figure 27.*
*Apple slices that are about ½-inch thick work best in a pie. We
found that peeling, quartering, and then removing the core from
each piece was most convenient. At this point, cut each quarter
into three wedges that should measure about ½-inch thick.*

*Figure 28.*
*If you cover your grater with waxed paper before grating*
*lemon zest, the zest will remain on top of the waxed paper*
*rather than clogging the grater's holes.*

*chapter nine*

# YULE LOG CAKE

ALLED BÛCHE DE NOËL IN FRANCE, A YULE log cake is a festive way to celebrate Christmas or other winter holidays. This impressive dessert is not nearly as difficult to prepare as it might seem. A yule log cake is nothing more than a fancy jelly roll cake with some meringue mushrooms for decoration. We tested every variable and developed a recipe that eliminates unnecessary steps and delivers foolproof results.

A yule log cake starts with a yellow sponge cake that's soft and moist but sturdy enough to be rolled. Many classic sponge cakes roll beautifully but can be tough and dry. We wanted a more tender, cakey crumb. Adding butter makes the cake fragile and difficult to roll. We found that whipping whole eggs gives the cake the desired lightness and that brushing it with brandy when cooled keeps it moist.

The cooled sponge cake is then spread with a thick, rich, light-colored buttercream (we like coffee here) and rolled up into a spiral. The cake is then covered with chocolate buttercream and decorated with meringue mushrooms. While many buttercream recipes start with confectioners' sugar, egg yolks, and butter, we found that powdered sugar results in a grainy texture, and dull color and flavor. A hot sugar syrup leaves behind no grittiness and because it does not contain any starch, it does not dull the flavor or color of the chocolate.

The same buttercream base can be used to make both the coffee and chocolate frostings for the inside and outside of the roll. Running the tines of a fork through the exterior buttercream imitates the rough texture of bark; slicing a piece off the roll and then attaching it to the top of the log creates a bump. Save extra buttercream for attaching the stems and caps of the meringue mushrooms, which are not essential but do make an attractive garnish.

# Yule Log Cake

➤ **NOTE:** *The buttercream and meringue mushrooms require the making of a sugar syrup heated to 238 degrees, the soft ball stage. Use a candy or instant-read thermometer for the greatest accuracy. Or, drizzle some of the syrup into a bowl of cold water and try to shape it with your fingertips. If syrup forms a soft ball, it has reached correct temperature. This recipe serves twelve.*

## Buttercream

|     |                                                 |
| --- | ----------------------------------------------- |
| ¾   | cup sugar                                       |
| 8   | egg yolks                                       |
| ¾   | pound (3 sticks) unsalted butter, at room temperature |
| ½   | teaspoon vanilla extract                        |
| 12  | ounces bittersweet chocolate, melted            |
| 1½  | tablespoons instant espresso powder             |
| 2   | teaspoons boiling water                         |

## Sponge Cake

|     |                                                 |
| --- | ----------------------------------------------- |
| 1   | tablespoon unsalted butter, at room temperature |
| 1   | cup plain cake flour                            |
| 1   | teaspoon baking powder                          |
| ¼   | teaspoon salt                                   |
| 3   | large eggs                                      |
| 1   | cup sugar                                       |
| 1   | teaspoon vanilla extract                        |
| 1   | tablespoon brandy or Cognac                     |

**78**

Meringue Mushrooms (*see* page 88)
Unsweetened cocoa powder
Confectioners' sugar

I N S T R U C T I O N S :

**1.** To make buttercream, combine ½ cup water and sugar in small, heavy saucepan. Cover and bring to boil over medium-high heat. Boil, swirling pan once or twice, until sugar has dissolved, 1 to 2 minutes. If necessary, wash down any sugar crystals on side of pan with damp pastry brush. Cook, uncovered, until temperature on thermometer registers 238 degrees, about 10 minutes.

**2.** While syrup is cooking, place egg yolks in large bowl of standing mixer fitted with wire whisk attachment. Beat at medium-high speed until pale yellow and very thick, about 5 minutes. With mixer at medium speed, slowly pour hot syrup into egg yolks, avoiding wire whisk. Continue to beat until mixture cools to room temperature, 5 to 10 minutes. Add butter 1 tablespoon at a time until all butter is thoroughly incorporated. Add vanilla.

**3.** Transfer one-third of buttercream to another bowl. Stir melted chocolate into first bowl of buttercream. Dissolve instant espresso in boiling water and stir into plain buttercream. Set both buttercreams aside at room temperature for up to 2 hours. (Buttercreams can be covered and refrigerated for 2 days or frozen for 1 week.)

**4.** Adjust oven rack to middle position and preheat oven to 375 degrees. Grease 16-by-11-inch jelly roll pan with 1 tablespoon butter. Line pan with parchment paper.

**5.** Sift flour with baking powder and salt; set aside. Place eggs in large bowl of standing mixer fitted with wire whisk attachment. Beat at medium-high speed until pale yellow and very thick, about 5 minutes. Slowly add sugar, then ⅓ cup water and vanilla. Add flour mixture and beat at medium speed until smooth, about 2 minutes. Pour batter into prepared pan, spread with spatula into corners, and rap pan once against counter to settle batter. Bake until cake layer is lightly browned and springs back when touched, 12 to 15 minutes.

**6.** Run knife along rim of pan to loosen cake. Cover top of cake with piece of parchment paper, then cover completely with large, damp kitchen towel. Place flat side of baking sheet on top of towel. Flip over both pans and lift off baking pan with cake. Carefully peel off top piece of parchment paper.

**7.** Position cake so that long side faces you. Fold bottom edge of towel and parchment paper over bottom edge of cake (*see* figure 29). Tightly roll cake (*see* figure 30, page 82) and set aside, seam side down, to cool for 30 minutes. Steady cake on either side with small bowl.

**8.** If buttercream has been refrigerated, bring to room temperature. Assemble and serve cake as directed in figures 31 through 37, page 82.

*Figure 29.*
*With kitchen towel and piece of parchment paper underneath cake layer, fold bottom edge of the towel over the long edge of the cake.*

*Figure 30.*

*Tightly roll the cake in the towel and set aside, seam side down, for 30 minutes. Steady cake on either side with small bowl. Rolling the cake while still warm will "train" it to roll without cracking when it cools.*

*Figure 31.*

*When the cake has cooled, unroll and peel off top piece of parchment paper. Sprinkle top of cake evenly with brandy. Spread evenly with coffee buttercream, leaving ⅛–inch border around edges uncovered.*

**82**

*Figure 32.*

*Roll cake in tight spiral, using towel to guide cake into proper shape. Separate parchment paper from bottom of cake as you roll.*

*Figure 33.*

Place a serrated knife 2 inches in from one end of the roll and cut
a diagonal slice. Set slice aside to make stump. Trim 1-inch slice
from other end of roll and discard.

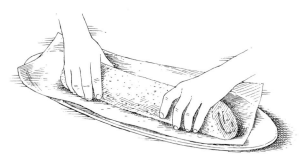

*Figure 34.*

Line serving platter with two 2-inch-wide strips of parchment
paper. (Parchment strips should be spaced about 2 inches apart
and will help keep platter clean as you apply the frosting.)
Center cake, seam side down, over strips.

**84**

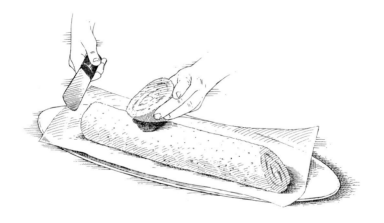

*Figure 35.*
*Place dab of chocolate buttercream several inches in from one end*
*of the roll. Place reserved slice of cake, flat side down, over*
*buttercream and attach to top of log.*

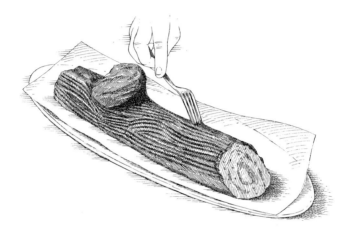

*Figure 36.*

*Spread exterior of cake, including stump but keeping ends clean, with thin layer of chocolate buttercream. Refrigerate cake until buttercream is firm, about 15 minutes. Apply thicker final coat of buttercream. (Reserve extra buttercream for assembling mushrooms.) Run tines of fork along the length of the cake to imitate bark. Carefully remove strips of parchment paper. At this point the cake can be refrigerated overnight or frozen for up to 1 month. Cover unfrosted ends with small piece of plastic wrap to protect them from drying out. If freezing, refrigerate until buttercream is firm and then wrap entire log in plastic.*

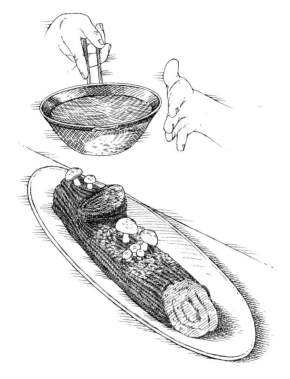

*Figure 37.*

When ready to serve, lightly sift cocoa powder over meringue
mushrooms and arrange mushrooms around cake on platter.
Sift confectioners' sugar lightly over cake and serve immediately.

# Meringue Mushrooms

➤ **NOTE:** *If the caps and stems become soggy during storage, crisp them in a 200-degree oven for 30 minutes before assembling the mushrooms. Make sure to save some extra chocolate buttercream for attaching caps and stems.*

½ cup plus 2 tablespoons sugar
2 large egg whites
pinch salt
⅛ teaspoon cream of tartar
½ teaspoon vanilla extract

**INSTRUCTIONS:**

**1.** Adjust oven racks to center and low positions and preheat oven to 200 degrees. Line two jelly roll pans with parchment paper.

**2.** Combine ¼ cup water and sugar in small, heavy saucepan. Cover and bring to boil over medium-high heat. Boil, swirling pan once or twice, until sugar has dissolved, 1 to 2 minutes. If necessary, wash down any sugar crystals on side of pan with damp pastry brush. Cook, uncovered, until temperature on thermometer registers 238 degrees, about 10 minutes.

**3.** While syrup is cooking, place egg whites in large bowl of standing mixer fitted with wire whisk attachment. Beat at medium-low speed until frothy, about 1 minute. Add salt and cream of tartar and beat, gradually increasing speed to high, to soft peaks, about 1 minute.

**4.** With mixer at medium speed, slowly pour hot syrup into egg whites, avoiding wire whisk. Increase speed to medium-high speed and continue to beat until meringue cools to room temperature and becomes very thick and shiny, 5 to 10 minutes. Add vanilla.

**5.** Fit pastry bag with ¼-inch pastry tip and fill with meringue. Pipe caps and stems onto paper-lined pans (*see* figures 38 and 39, page 90).

**6.** Bake meringue for 2 hours, turn off oven, and let rest in oven until very dry and crisp, about 30 minutes longer. Cool mushroom caps and stems on pans. (Store in airtight container for up to 1 week.) To assemble mushrooms, use buttercream to "glue" caps and stems together (*see* figures 40 and 41, page 92).

*Figure 38.*

*Holding bag about ¼ inch above paper, pipe 30 rounds of vary-
ing sizes to form mushroom caps. Keep the tip steady as the
meringue flows into a round shape, stopping the pressure when
the desired size is reached. To release the meringue without making a point, turn the tip clockwise and lift the bag straight up. If
pointed tip forms, dip finger into a bowl of cold water and gently
smooth the top of the cap to remove the tip.*

*Figure 39.*

*To shape mushroom stems, hold pastry bag perpendicular to the
pan, almost touching the paper. Force meringue through tip as
you pull up on the bag. The stems should be about 1-inch tall and
stand up straight. Pointed ends are desired so just stop squeezing
bag as you lift it straight up.*

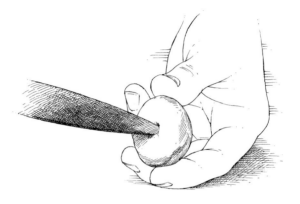

*Figure 40.*
*Use a small paring knife or skewer to make an indentation in*
*the underside of each mushroom cap.*

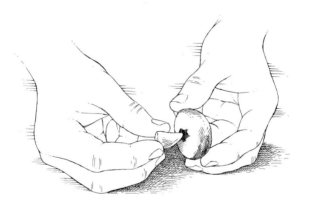

*Figure 41.*
*Use tip of knife or toothpick to place a small dot of buttercream*
*into the hole in each cap and onto the tip of each stem. Gently*
*press the cap onto the end of the stem.*

# *i n d e x*

All-Season Apple Pie, **70**

Apple Pie with Dried Fruit, **73**

Chocolate Soufflé, **56**

Classic Trifle, **22**

Cranberry Apple Pie, **73**

Crème Brûlée, **64**

Crystallized Ginger Apple Pie, **73**

Easy Chocolate Truffles, **36**

Fluffy Orange-Mace Hard Sauce, **53**

Fresh Raspberry Puree, **31**

Ginger Crème Brûlée, **66**

Lemon Whipped Cream, **32**

Make-Ahead Soufflé, **58**

Meringue Mushrooms, **88**

Mocha Soufflé, **58**

Modern Mincemeat Pie, **12**

Plum Pudding, **46**

Pumpkin Crème Brûlée, **66**

Rich Baked Custard, **30**

Sponge Sheet Cake, **28**

Yule Log Cake, **78**